Wild Juice

Southern Messenger Poets

Dave Smith, *Series Editor*

Wild Juice

Poems

Ashley Mace Havird

Louisiana State University Press

Baton Rouge

Published by Louisiana State University Press
www.lsupress.org

LSU Press Paperback Original

Designer: Laura Roubique Gleason
Typefaces: Minion Pro, text; Bodoni OS, display

The author would like to thank the editors of the following journals for publishing the poems noted, sometimes in earlier versions: *American Journal of Poetry*: "Advent," "Earth Day," and "The Hound"; *Bayou*: "1939: Adoptive Mother"; *Chautauqua Literary Journal*: "Babyland" and "Diving before Dawn"; *Cold Mountain Review*: "Ghost Net," "Golden Dawn," and "Tour of Grief"; *Crab Orchard Review*: "Fifty" and "Late for Reading, 1959"; *Cumberland River Review*: "Migrant Worker" and "Proof"; *Fleur de Lit*: "Perseids"; *Hodge Podge Poetry*: "Hand-Knit"; *Image*: "Strays"; *LEON Literary Review*, "Beach Music"; *Literary Matters*: "Bone Pit," "Dementia: American Pickers," "Habitat," "Skull Mount," "Suitcase," "Turtle and Snake," and "Waterline"; *Louisiana English Journal*: "The Sale" and "Vernix"; *Nola Diaspora*: "Gone to Wild"; *Sewanee Review*: "First Year"; *Slant*: "Yellow Dog"; *South Carolina Review*: "Fixing Junior"; *Southern Humanities Review*: "The Gardener."
    Grateful thanks to the Shreveport Regional Arts Council for its invaluable support.
    Deepest appreciation to Julie Kane and Ava Leavell Haymon for their encouragement and suggestions; Dave Smith, for his patience and expertise during the final revisions of some of these poems; and David Havird, with whom many of these poems represent a true collaboration.

Cover photograph by Edith Irvine, 1896. (Color added.) Courtesy Edith Irvine Collection, L. Tom Perry Special Collections, Harold B. Lee Library, Brigham Young University.

Library of Congress Cataloging-in-Publication Data

Names: Havird, Ashley Mace, author.
Title: Wild juice : poems / Ashley Mace Havird.
Description: Baton Rouge : Louisiana State University Press, [2021] | Series: Southern messenger poets | "LSU Press Paperback Original"—Title page verso.
Identifiers: LCCN 2020028536 (print) | LCCN 2020028537 (ebook) | ISBN 978-0-8071-7473-9 (paperback) | ISBN 978-0-8071-7523-1 (pdf) | ISBN 978-0-8071-7524-8 (epub)
Subjects: LCGFT: Poetry.
Classification: LCC PS3608.A88235 W55 2021 (print) | LCC PS3608.A88235 (ebook) | DDC 811/.6—dc23
LC record available at https://lccn.loc.gov/2020028536
LC ebook record available at https://lccn.loc.gov/2020028537

For my father, Bob Mace

Contents

This Unhealing

Phantom Limbs

Wild Juice

Skull Mount

Clean-shot, it should have dropped. The deer
trailed blood thirty yards. My nephew tracked
his kill to the bank of the brown water-grave
of the swamp. With his dad hauled it home
in the bed of the Polaris. Eight points.
What struck me was how fast, how far from life
it had come. Congealed blood stuck like a fat tick
to the bottom lip, eyes dry as paper, nostrils still.
"Remember Walter? Used to be
I'd take him venison," my brother, Scott,
is saying, "and he would clean our rifles.
Didn't hunt, though—fished."
And Robert, my nephew, as if on cue:
"What do you call a fish with no eyes?" His joke
since he was five. "Fssshhh," he grins,
his boy's head now atop a six-foot frame.

How had I never before *looked*?
Years on the farm. Brothers who hunted.
Why this Christmas, the one without our father?
A week's gathering there in the house
where we grew up. Sasanquas, now roof-high,
laid fuchsia blankets over the brown grass.
Come night, Cold Moon. Full
frost-silvering moon of my girlhood.
Our father refused to hunt. But how he praised
my brothers' kills—the mallard's emerald head,
the turkey's crimson wattle, the deer's broad rack—
then put on jazz and turned up the volume.

Butchering done, beside the bone pit, Scott
goes at the spine with a hacksaw
beneath the skull. In the backyard,
water set to boil over propane. It takes all day
to scald away skin and flesh. A twisted wire

scrambles, hooks out the brain.
It takes a case of Bud Light, chain-smoked
Marlboros, a barrage of hunting stories,
around the steaming pot. Two more days
in a pan of bleach. One day to dry in the sun.
With a toothbrush, peroxide (Clairol, No. 40)
where bone meets bone. A bubbling.
I can't get enough of looking.

Most days toward the end my brother
drove our father in the mud-splattered Polaris
down dirt roads alongside fields,
through timber and into the cypress swamps,
his life's landscape. It never failed,
according to Scott—that fallen-in shack
where pasture met woods tricked time.
A boy again, our father, along with his father,
lays those pine floorboards for Walter,
our cowman who loved his horse, but never
a woman. On a salvaged pine slab
that knew our father's hands and knees,
my brother mounts the skull. Hangs it
in the dated kitchen, against the wallpaper's
floral mauve. Beside the cuckoo clock,
which nobody now troubles to wind.

Gone to Wild

Homo naledi

September 2015

From NPR, good news! A Link,
long-lost relative, in the buckets of bone
threaded sunward from that deep-
African cave, Chamber of Stars.
Ritual burial, millions of years ago. *Millions.*
Until now, inconceivable.
Paleontologists are giddy.
Skull, jaw, rib, even inner-ear bones.
Feet that could "wear our Nikes."
Long curved fingers just made for football.

I rethink cremation. If I were to rest
entire, say, in the bed of the Red River,
I, too, might be reborn in a mega-annum—
why not? My bones counted, coveted,
perhaps pocketed for luck,
studied for anything they might reveal—
hours hunched, tensed, over mobile devices;
a cocktail of poisons banked
from microwaving leftovers in plastic
and bingeing on Cheetos;
osteoarthritis in my knees, hips, toes. . . .

In hushed tones, to be the object,
as future *Homo whatever*s brush silt
from my stained fragments, of infinite
supposing: *Artist? Priestess? Mother—*
Our Mother?
How completely I might rise,
again stand on my bone-spurred
all-too-human feet—recovered!
All they imagine me to be.

Yearly Physical

I'd rather be a child and sit Indian-style.
The brisk nurse asks me my age.
Can't she read?
The clipboard in her membraned
hand surely reveals my DOB
in permanent ink. Exposed
beneath this sheet of paper,
I gaze at the jar of Popsicle sticks.
Oh, for the days when a flattened
tongue was my greatest fear!

Out in the waiting room an old woman,
hair bobbed ragged, her wheelchair smack
in the middle of facing seats. Babbling,
she's trying to learn her words again.
A pimpled teenage girl, mouth open,
watches her like TV. A tiny boy
picks at her lap robe until
one dancing eye picks *him*.
Beside me a tight perm nets the bald spot
of a head cupped in blue-veined hands. . . .
I tried to focus
on the sunken-cheeked waif-models
of Milan in *Elle,* leapt up
at my mispronounced name.

Each spring I return
to this small stark room
with its pocked ceiling and vinyl walls
and am closer to the day, no doubt
in April, for this is my time,
when someone—a trained aide?—
will have license to thrust me
center-stage, a fabulous child
on show for the waiting others.

The Gardener

My husband can't stop watching
the woman who can't stop gardening
across the street. She's fortyish,
like me, but blonde, which is better,
and newly divorced.
"I've never seen her up close."
No masking his frustrated lust.

She *is* distant,
but once, crossing the street,
she handed me a bunch of limp four o'clocks.
They'd take over a bed, she warned,
if I didn't watch out.

She's blonde. Did I mention that?
Loose-limbed as a teenager and lovely,
if you can forgive her eyes, focused
on a face rarer than yours—
lavender moonflower or bearded iris.
And she's passionate, judging from her spells
of ravenous pruning.

Hers is a jumble of a garden—
Shasta, daylily, gardenia, rose, canna.
It flatters her house, its gables
and pitched roof,
arched windows that reveal
a huge rack of antlers and a caged cockatiel.

How could I not prefer it
to this solid Georgian,
its staid azaleas and family portraits
shot at three-year intervals?
There I could grow wild
and—who knows?—even beautiful.

Gone to Wild

Not like young folk—manic kids or feverish teenagers—
but old women, those I knew back when I wasn't one.
Great-Aunt Millie, "the pretty sister," my grandmother sniffed.
Sly-eyed, secrets pushing to sprout from her tight-lipped smile,
her cheek to my kiss a pollen-dusted rose.
Or my best friend's thin too-friendly Aunt Irene,
teeth stained red (her lipstick wandered),
whose fingertips, new-growth tendrils of jasmine,
grazed our arms if we got too close.

Or the ones whose names I've long forgotten—
cousins twice, thrice, who knows how many times removed—
who never missed reunions at Antioch Baptist Church.
Dressed to the nines in sky blue, peach, mint green, lilac,
hair spun and sprayed into fine and fluffy clouds,
they won all the door prizes: Oldest Descendant,
Traveled Farthest, Perfect Attendance.
Chatting among themselves, notes rising, falling,
depending on whether or not they wanted you to hear.
Tearing up generously, equally, at drooling babies
and toppled headstones in the gone-to-wild graveyard.

I picture them rooted, both garden and gardeners,
pruning, feeding, clawing up weeds in a fury.
Their perfume reeled me in.
Arms strong from the hoe—how else to explain such force?—
squeezed me to stalk-stiff corset or peony-cushioned bosom.
They weren't about to let go.

Reading the Trees

I go for a walk. My dog goes to school—
at the sinewy base of a crape myrtle,
a brick wall thick with jasmine,
the chain-link between a howling basset
and the traffic on Highland Avenue.
He reads vertically and with great depth
of understanding—or so I imagine—
past bark to the very core of the oak.
The tip of his black nose quivers
and drips into pom-poms of liriope,
the marigolds beneath a Coldwell Banker's
swinging SOLD. What he learns
is always news, in disappearing ink.
Each morning the Labrador fetches
from my dew-drenched lawn
the *Times,* whose news is hardly indelible,
its lines of print bleeding into each other.
He drops it at my feet. "Not much there,"
his gray-chinned sigh seems to declare.

Perseids

Worley Observatory, August 2015

The hard-lit steel plant to the east
muddies the strict dark of the fields.
Where else to run away from home to but here,
this observatory that small-town dreamers
built atop a corncrib. Relic like us—Dorie and me—
of the '60s, it draws dreamers still,
hoping for a spectacle.
Conditions are as good as they get.
No moon, few clouds, even a breeze
to break the heat. Some stranger—
amateur astronomer?—says look to the west,
be patient, releases us to be girls,
to lie flat on dry grass, to watch the sky
for what comes: blinking planes, satellite flares,
heat lightning, the Milky Way . . . constellations
whose names we don't know, so we invent them—
Sherpa, Boaz—black dogs we mourn. Patience?
We have the patience of girls pole-fishing
with grandfathers deep in swamps,
girls whose stiff-fingered grandmothers spin yarns
endless as galaxies. We have the patience
to pray hard for a miracle.
Slash of a meteor so near, so bright, we startle.
Burned out too fast, too soon, even for a wish.

The Sale

She's out in the garage
when dusk stretches violet cellophane
over the bowl of her world.
Except there is a gash
for the moon to shine through.
And fireflies dance beneath it.

She turns to her work,
this junk that nobody wants.
But somebody will.
A buck for this, a buck
for that. People will buy anything
for a buck.
Even this burnt-orange ottoman
with cigarette holes,
this vintage avocado blender
bearing crusty evidence from the '70s
of her failed spinach soufflé,
the turtle sandbox whose eyes her children
gouged once they outgrew it,
that gaudy ceramic rooster
(long-closeted wedding gift),
a fat happy family of Japanese figurines.

Surely this much is hers,
her family's leftovers. Surely
she can do with them what she wants,
even if it means selling out.

Silver Plate

Their station is far above me,
beyond my reach on the pantry's topmost shelf.
Thick with tarnish, sooty as cast-iron:
serving trays—ovals and rectangles,
plain and embossed. *Vintage.* Nesting
Revere bowls, pitchers big and small,
a score of julep cups, candy saucers galore.

How they gleamed when jewelry-store
new, and I was new-married twenty.
They mirrored my uncomplicated face.
Now black with judgment, they've grown into themselves.
For that, they don't forgive. Gavel down. *Guilty.*
My glance rises to meet their burnt-out eyes.
*Remember that girl doing her best with rag
and paste? You took me in—remember?*

To show good faith, I order Blitz. "Since 1912."
Five stars from Amazon, the best!
that nonetheless requires "elbow grease."
I come to my senses. All this for a thin rind
of precious-over-base metal with,
experts agree, "no intrinsic silver value"?

You'll never be sterling, my friends,
nor even, again, buffed mirrors of plate,
your black look Blitzed away, while there
is forming my own patina of sensible lines.

Vernix

The second you step out the door,
it coats you like vernix. How,
exactly, to breathe this spore-thick haze?

Red wasps fire up the St. Augustine.
Yellow jackets patrol the sidewalk.
You have to watch your step.

Wisteria reaches, too familiar
with legs and arms. Muffled as though underwater,
jays chainsaw the pines.

Oak shade, musty as Grandma's forbidden closets.
Bulbous toadstools rise like sea sponges
from the mossy root bed.

Sweat stings your eyes,
as the sun muscles down,
closing in on Louisiana in late August.

You pray for baptism,
storm that hurls summer like a coconut—
bursts of milky rain.

Vanishing Act

Diving before Dawn

Over your eyes, clearer eyes.
Over your skin, thicker skin.
Your breath heavy on your back
until the sea lifts it and lowers you
as though you are a small child
onto the silt floor.
Open your light. Find what it finds.

Parrotfish in crevices levitate in spun clouds
of their own making. Filefish rest
motionless in fingers of sea rods,
turtles drift in a sunken tugboat's hull.
The night garden grows.
Anemones open like hands of newborns.
Purple sponges glow as though lit from within.
Coral blooms all over itself. . . .
It is the time of the night-hunters.
Octopi pulse their sacs of greenish light.
Morays, mouths agape, prowl the reef.
Silvery tarpon sidle up and follow your beam
to small sleepers. A snapper
snaps down a damselfish.

Outside your circle of light,
shapes take shape.
Luminescence sparks blue.
The parrotfish stirs, shakes off its cocoon
which thins away in your slow-motion hands.
Dawn filters down. Tiny spiderlike shrimp
groom an open-mouthed grouper.
For half a breath, a pair of banded butterflies—
still-life above a yellow tube sponge.
Now, all is motion. Schools of sergeant majors,
blue tang, chromis. Tagalong angels,
trumpets, durgons. Day-hunters.

Near surface, silversides open their curtain,
deliver you to the sun-hard world
of your weight on feet. Flat walls
at right angles, voices, machines.

Tour of Grief

Heat waves, wildfires . . . Waves
of migrants, children ripped from parents—
their blankets of glittering foil.

Polar thaw . . . and the slick
curve of a whale's black back,
her laboring spout—beside her head,

small dorsal fin. A killer whale
with her dead calf. Tahlequah.
With forehead and fin

nudging the calf to the surface.
Floating it there on her rostrum.
Clutching its tail in her mouth.

The calf breathed long enough
for milk to come, for it to nurse,
for her to bond. Its blowhole sputtered. Flukes

fell still. In spite of currents, waves—
Tahlequah, Two
Together. How human her grief seems,

even scientists marvel.
With trills and clicks and whistles,
other whales in the pod

offer the rare,
once plentiful Chinook.
Ease the calf away,

float it themselves. How human.
Seventeen days,
one thousand miles.

Only when a thrumming, like breath,
wings from the calf's slack jaw—
a plume of flies—does she release it. . . .

Heat waves, wildfires, polar thaw,
ocean of glittering foil.
A mass of high pressure, which weather maps

color the Indian Red
of my childhood's crayons,
squatting over the West.

Advent

Sandy Hook, December 14, 2012

No longer afraid of the dark,

twenty first-graders lie
in strange deep rooms, while snug

in their own beds, solid citizens
load in their sleep

where not a whimper in swaddling clothes
disturbs their steel-cold grip,

while out in the dark
others, addled, howl

to the nightlight crescent moon,
their soft palms warmed by panting fur.

Specially trained dogs nuzzled the children
with luck who lived.

Golden Dawn

To this day
(the Athens taxi driver said),
my father has a hole in his head
from a Nazi boot. He was crawling
on his belly under a fence
to reach some garbage.
He was that hungry.
The soldier kicked him.
The toe of the boot was metal.
My father was nine.
Just last week a woman sat in my cab
where you are sitting.
She was seventy years or more.
The Nativist Party would fix everything,
she said, rid the streets
of migrants with dark skin
who soil the sidewalks, who steal
from decent Greek people.
She talked and talked.
The more she talked, the more
I wanted to drag her out of my car
and strangle her. But I would stay
for the rest of my life in prison. That
I could not do—not with children,
a wife. So, I strangled myself.

Late for Reading, 1959

Skinny second-grade sharecropper boys:
straw-headed, lizard-eyed, sores scratched open.
Nehi for supper, Baby Ruth for lunch.
Cussing already. They run in packs.

They drink no milk. They eat no peas.

First week of first grade. I don't know
the ropes. Past swings, coal pile,
whitewashed gym—I've gone too far.
Red apple half-eaten in my hand.

They brush no teeth.

Heavy-sweet hedge, honeysuckle
to pluck to touch to tongue-tip. First bell.
Yellow jackets swarm the bitten apple,
apple dropped before it stings.

They kiss no mother.

Three—long-legged, too fast.
Cheek fisted down, mouth spitting grit.
Up my dress, ragged nails dig past elastic.
Last bell rings. I'm late for Reading.

They live in dust. Find home in fields.

Fifty

Child with the lost name, it was your skin
that stood you with the others at the barn
working our tobacco, when the tractor,
through heavy morning fog, towed in a drag
stacked with cropped green leaves for curing.
It nudged the pole that held the roof.
And the pole felled you.
Skin whiskey brown as Catfish Creek.

Come afternoon my father's jittery hands
gripped his Super 8. Preserved for posterity
the ringlets, crinoline, back-bowed sashes
of my birthday party. Off to one side
Mattie in her good uniform, face behind her hands.
No word uttered about what happened
down by the swamp. Ten candles sputter out.
Jesse leads in the horse I'd begged for.
It fills the frame.

Forty years later to the day, my father,
after one too many stiff ones, unearths you,
without a name, whose life I cannot find
in my own, though I search in my mind
reel after reel, frame by frame.
Those were the days before people knew
about suing folks for a fortune.
He paid for your funeral. Sent flowers.
Even visited your family, even sat in your house.

Name? Honey, that was a long time ago.
He believes you were ten, like me.
Happen nowadays—he knocks back the Jack—
I'd be sued in a snap.

Sheltering My Father

Three Old Snapshots in Black-and-White

Everything soft and gray and blurry like you need glasses . . . No
way to hold it still, my Kodak Brownie. Our front yard, Easter,
early '60s. There you are, so young in your dark suit, fedora, wide-
striped tie. Your hand raised, palm out—enough! Pecan tree still
leafless. Its shadow gropes new grass, pale fence, daffodils broken
into bloom. Your easy grin tells me that Mama hasn't told you what
I told her. About him.

Date: May 1967. Place: water's edge, Surfside Beach. You stand
behind Mama, your arms around her. Her head turned, she smiles
a tight smile, eyes hidden behind dark cat-eye glasses. A cigarette
between her fingers. Your hatless profile as you admire her movie-
star face wears the receding hairline my younger brother inherited.
My uncle, her brother, might have been what people used to call
"funny," but he sure as hell took great shots.

This one, too. We're standing in a doorway, you and I. Dark wood
paneling. Something white looms behind us—a refrigerator? I'm
thirteen, maybe fourteen. I fit just under your shoulder, where
you think I am safe. The pocket of your plaid shirt holds a Cross
pen-and-pencil set; you were big on those. Hat pushed to the back
of your head, you look to the left, your eyes glazed, your thoughts
elsewhere. I look to the right. Anywhere but at the camera.

Operation

My father lay upon steel
nine hundred miles east,
his chest sliced open.
I knelt in dirt among bright pansies,
pinching off each wilted face.

I'd never felt so far from home,
not even while hiking in '86
the snow-patched mountains of Norway,
slightly radioactive
from the Chernobyl meltdown.

When it was over, my brother phoned:
A tumor the size of a tangerine.

I can see it no other way
than glowing,
a deep orange fruit whose squat lobes
deliver the juice of suns
to thaw our winter table.

In the family photograph
shot last summer at midday,
we all squint. My father's bare head,
bald and fringed in white,
ghosts upward into light.

1939: My Father's Adoptive Mother

Already she sees a ghost in the clouds
of her mirror. Hidden, a tumor
where should have grown a child.

In lamplight she unbuttons the stiff
neck of her blouse. Her fingers catch
on her throat's strong pulse.

Her belly still flat as a girl's.
Her dark skirt, a heavy pool
snagging her feet.

Auburn waves reach midback. Shorn,
they will coil in a cigar box,
for her boy to touch to his cheek

at bedtime. Eleven, half-teasing:
what do women *look* like?
His friends spoke of pictures.

For life, she will fix the son
of her choosing within a frame,
the door of her image.

Picturing herself a statue, an angel—
the statue of an angel, a figure she's seen—
she opens the door, steps out.

Babyland

Sleep-weary, they grew
weary too of looking for their sheep
among these slabs
like small wrapped gifts that rhyme—
Boy Blue, Bo-Peep—the same
two scenes laid down time and again
around their Babyland's pavilion.
Infant . . . But most have names,
gently used. Their days recorded.
No room for Mother, Father,
compelled to leave and leave and leave.

These little ones once knew tears.
Now they know rain.
Your eyes rain-blurred,
it's easy to picture them, filmy shapes
among rabbits, robins, squirrels.
Barefoot they run in puddles,
swarm the heavy oaks, swim the ponds,
crawl into the cold arms of angels.
All the grassy acres of Forest Park,
theirs—for play and play and play.

The game of Names.
A favorite, even for the littlest ones
whose eyes never opened,
whose frail fingers have learned to read
the important upright stones like braille:
Eatwell Skeeters. Hasty Eatman.
Goode Patient. The combinations—endless.
Hipple Hyde. Payne, Gore, and *Stump.* Nearby,
the bones of the long-lived dead wear toothy smiles,
the tedium of waiting for resurrection
thank God interrupted.

Soldier Boy

The motorcycle I pretended not
to hate, the reel-to-reel that lobbed
Jimi and Janis from wall to wall—bare rooms,
second floor of a rented farmhouse.
Mexican crucifix over your bed
where you never crossed the line
but boxed me up like a saint's anklebone.

Years flying helicopters over Vietnam—
you never wanted to talk about them.
In school again, you kept trying to fit
back into *boy,* as though it was a favorite pair
of jeans, outgrown. Kept trying to eat meat
again: pressed towels into T-bones—red handprints
on white cotton—before charring them.

Nights under stars at the foot
of the Blue Ridge, what did you hear
in the hoarse waves of crickets? The Big Twin
of your Harley gunning us west?
My girl, you'd hum. I conjured, eastward,
the spangled Atlantic, crumple of breakers, tide
retreating. I was already leaving.

A Sort of Prayer

In second grade we copied in No. 2 lead
simple drawings and the names beneath:
egg, caterpillar, cocoon, butterfly or moth.
No crayons allowed. For stern Miss Brown,
miracles were rote. One recess

she netted a swallowtail, with polished nails
pinched its body still. Laid it upon toxic cotton
in a jar labeled "Kill." Screwed tight the lid.
Before last bell, tweezed out and sandwiched
between small panes what was now artifact.
I hadn't yet learned the magic words
to bring it back to life: *Chrysalis. Pupa. Instar. . . .*
How astonishing, bizarre!—the way the body
liquifies, transfigures its very cells, then rises
born-again, *metamorphosed,* as swallowtail.

Hemolymph: the stuff pumped into wrinkled
newborn wings. Hours spent slow-fanning
(a sort of prayer), easy pickings for robins, wrens,
until the black velvet dries, expands
jewel-trimmed, into the air.

I watch for days (a sort of prayer)
a litter of instars, white-mitted, arrayed
in stripes and spots of yellow, black, and green—
devouring my potted parsley, molting,
eating their skins, losing their heads, pug-faced—
minting emerald nuggets of waste.

Grandmother Faceless

That runaway bay with side-wild eyes,
herself a girl bareback, fearless,
fingers knotting the rough mane.
Cypress swamps where she shot turtles
off logs for luck and caught enough catfish
to feed six brothers and a baby sister.
Once outran an alligator. . . .

At dawn she rolled from her feather bed
where we two traded sleep for stories
winter nights when my parents went out.
Now, she said, *I must put on my face.*
I knew what she meant, but still, to think
I'd lain in the center's sunken V
all night amid fumes of Vicks VapoRub,
her soft flesh sliding loose like meringue
from the slick skim of her lemon tarts,
with a woman without a face.

I watched her, efficient
beside the electric fire, firm herself
inside girdle, brassiere, stockings, slip.
Then, bent toward her dresser mirror,
smear, pat, and blot from an array of pots.
Base and powder, lipstick and rouge.
Sensible dress, earbobs, shoes that laced.
Sprayed gray finger waves.
She taught fifth grade. Only in first,
I would have to face the cold.
Not yet that white glass jar
marked "Vanishing Cream." Thank God,
not yet the mirror.

Wreck

That's when Mama put her foot down.
My brothers and I would never again
ride with Granddad if he
was behind the wheel. *Can you believe*
they let him keep his license?
He knew somebody—had to be.

It was a miracle, or so Mama said,
that we survived. I remember nothing.
Only the mangled, dusty blue Ford
in the junkyard stays with me—
the shape of my forehead, a mosaic bowl,
bulging from the windshield.

After years of surrendering her babies
in sun or miserable rain to this cigar-
chewing farmer, to check barns, feed cows,
walk timber, collect ticks, knowing
we'd get stuck in some pasture,
then soaked, then sick—

after the nightmare sight
of her children jouncing home
atop the cab of his pickup, feet dangling
over bug-splatted glass—
at last she would keep us safe.
The old fool would go alone now
wherever he had to go.

Hand-Knit

When I was five,
my grandmother owned the Atlantic,
its rim of beach.
Beneath a wide straw hat,
behind dark green glasses,
she stood waist-deep and opened her arms.
She held it back—the coaxing deep.

In my next life, she said,
I'm going to be a singer.
I believed her.
In this one she knitted, mended, sewed.
A command: *Be still.*
She commenced to pin my hems
into silver rings that pricked.

"Hand-Knit by Honey"
tagged the sweaters, hats,
Christmas stockings for me, my brothers,
their wives, my husband, and finally,
my child. This last one is childlike,
the crescent moon a crawfish dancing
above a cockeyed Santa.

I push up the sleeves
of my Fair-isle cardigan,
its pattern of leafy thistle. *Begin,*
slip together, increase, continue, repeat.
Her fingers cast, knit, purl around me.
Beside our lit fir, my small daughter
sings, twirling, eyes closed, arms out.

Beach Music

Myrtle Beach, 1966

Clear from the shell-pink-stucco-
with-turquoise-trim motel she managed
to the Pavilion Amusement Park,
my grandmother held my hand.

Convertibles blared down the boulevard:
Under the boardwalk . . . What kind of fool . . .
Ain't too proud to beg . . . Thirteen,
I flashed Vs for peace at soldiers on leave.

My too-long legs itched to run.
The air was charged with Krispy Kreme,
Coppertone, foot-longs, sea spray.
She squeezed my hand till it hurt

at the saltwater taffy machine
whose metal arms worked pastel ribbons,
its window framed with colored lights
reflecting her face lit up like a child's. *Stay,*

just a little bit longer . . .
We were so close to the rides,
I could hear the clack clack clack
of the roller coaster teasing up

its wooden scaffold—release so close—
the screaming plunge.

This Unhealing

Dementia: *American Pickers*

2 a.m. He's awake.
Don't need the walker hell no.
My brother catches him mid-fall.
For Dad, it's sunup. No matter we show him
the pitch dark outside, the clocks, our phones,
the four watches he's placed in a perfect row
on the kitchen table. Finally, he has enough
of us and our so-called truth.
You believe what you believe. I believe
what I believe. That shuts us up all right.
We make coffee. Camp out in the den,
let the always-day of TV take over.
One episode after another of *American Pickers.*
Mike and Frank, who take road trips and
bargain for "rusty gold" in the wilds of rural America
and sometimes cities, too. Lord, the stuff they find!
The crazy-as-a-fox backwoods folk they meet!
There's Lester the Taxidermist
with his stuffed miniature horse. Big Bear
and his World War Two samurai sword.
There's Goat Man and Mole Man and Hobo Jack.
Backyard shacks where Rock 'Em Sock 'Em Robots
lurk. *Planet of the Apes* lunchbox, pristine.
An honest-to-God dinosaur bone. Not to mention
a 10-foot fiberglass cowboy boot.
Sunup for real, my brother helps our father
to bed. The teepee with red handprints holds me,
this stage prop belonging to Iron Eyes Cody,
the "Crying Indian" from those early '70s
anti-littering commercials. Truth be told,
he was a Louisiana boy with Italian roots.
His tear was glycerin. I googled him.

Suitcase

I will, my father swears,
put your suitcase right here.
He pats the seat of his walker.
This night before I leave
he refuses to sleep for making plans.
I will take it to the car for you.
He's erased the impossible brick steps
down to the driveway.
I will drive you to the airport
(with or without a license).
Come morning he does none of these things.
He does only one thing.
I'll miss you, Shug. God knows,
I will. And he kisses my cheek.
And the bones of his shoulders meet my hands
through the thin cotton of his shirt.
Will he remember who I am
next time? Driving to catch my plane,
I feel myself, everything I packed, spilling,
spooling out. There's no next time.
I'm looking for the parts
of me he gathered and took with him.

Hospice: Adoptive Mother Who Died Young

We don't want him to spend nights
alone, so we take turns, my brothers and I.
Our father has made the trip back
to his first self, newborn in a crib
in a Home, perhaps not unlike this one,
for the motherless. She will come,
this legend—an angel, she seemed
when he described her to us—who chose
his curls, dimples, nut-brown eyes.
She would take care of him. A promise
for ten years kept, eighty deferred.
She's homemaking now,
with soup at a simmer, bread rising.
I wedge the sheet between mattress
and railing, tuck him in—my father,
who's hungry where she is
who's made a bed for her boy.

Hospice: Grace

It was nice for a death room.
Machines with blinking lights
to chart the journey,
adjustable bed with railings.
For us watchers, soft chairs,
pamphlets that pictured sunsets
(or maybe they were sunrises)
in an otherwise empty bookcase,
built-in drawers with pillows and sheets
for the extra bed that turned into a sofa
when the light came back. A window
with blinds that opened to June
green from the downpour
the night it was my turn to stay
the dark hours, the night I drove
in the storm to Wendy's and the girl
with sequined nails behind the counter
handed me a Frosty no charge
and did not lose patience
when I broke down and held up the line.

Turtle and Snake

I let go of his hand that stayed curled like a shell,
the hand I pretended was holding mine too,
took the dirt road toward the swamp.
At the edge of the field, to my left, a turtle.
To my right, a snake, five-footer, stick-straight.
Cottonmouth, if I wasn't mistaken.
Without thinking the thing through,
wanting nothing more than to *fix,*
I moved the turtle out into the tall green.
Then saw in the road the lip of loose sand,
the hole, the clutch. The snake,
it came to me (I'm a bit slow), was waiting.
Why, if it had to, it would wait all day.
I set the turtle back—tried to, anyhow—
the way she had been. I wanted to believe
she would blanket her eggs with soft dirt,
camouflage the nest, outwait the snake.
I walked on, hauling my hope like a heavy shell.

Daisy's Heart

Late afternoon and Daisy,
that Lab mix with a curled-up tail,
ran circles around us, leapt
into hayfields, the scrub that fringed the pines,
the snaky brown water of the swamp.
A two-year-old whose bad heart rendered her
all ribs, she raced through deep grass
the way she always did and beat us to the orchard.

We stopped near the gate, amazed by dragonflies.
At dusk they looked like birds almost,
or maybe bats, swooping and sweeping.
Their wings hummed. A continuation, it seemed,
of last night's alchemy: *a vision—no—a feeling,*
the moment he died, of something blasting apart,
sparks raining down. We turned. Lying in grass,
eyes open, she'd almost got to the house.

We buried her by the pickup's headlights,
while dark swarmed in from all sides
and mosquitoes drank the blood that pulsed to our skin.
Next day we buried our father's ashes
with those same shovels.

Deer

Where orchard meets hayfield, blueberry bushes
have dried to sticks. The berries, a countable few,
have shriveled. My brother planted them in sand,
in too much sun, no irrigation. Clouds
flame over the western pines. Two deer step out

from the pines. This morning I picked wildflowers,
yellow and purple—their names escape me.
And placed them over my father.
A kicked-up shard of Indian pottery, too,
from the farm, and a smooth white stone from Greece.

I described through the churchyard's shovel-tamped ground
the moonscape of Milos, the chalk-white shore
and indigo sea, and pictured his fingers alive,
sunned brown, curling around the stone. . . . The deer
hightail it, no matter the palmful of berries,

into the dusk of the woods. Tomorrow, I'll tell him
about the deer, how they caught my scent—and stood.

Prayer Flags

Before hauling them to Goodwill,
I hang my father's shirts in the order
of prayer flags beneath Mount Kailash,
where I've never been but can picture myself,
breath honed by cold stone air,
bendy from the altitude, equilibrium shot.
There—against the mountain's snow-dome
rising otherworldly into cerulean day
or night's Milky Way—this sky-blue chambray,
spittled with grease from the insides
of broke-down tractors;
the white dress oxford, long kept stiff
for tenor solos at weddings and funerals,
releasing its starch at last in the wind;
this red plaid flannel, sleeves pitted
by the wayward sparks of a December fire.
Yes, like my father who had no truck
with rest, they'll thin and fray and scatter.
Meanwhile, two for the price of one!
I picture that Kelly green knit,
sea salt-limp, trawling the Atlantic for king,
that mustard-yellow broadcloth,
shredded at collar and cuff, clearing
come spring a lawn of broken limbs.

First Year

Mine was a child's fall,
the hurt a mother or father can more or less fix
with Band-Aids, a kiss. Almost to the top
of the steep concrete steps to the gym,
my toe jammed. Caught my weight on stiff arms.
(Decent reflexes for sixty-three.) Spectacularly
bloody, my scraped-raw palms, skinned knees.
The healing, though! I was obsessed.
Hands held out, fingers splayed. Imagine:
all those invisible cells repairing.
First the shredded skin—it dried overnight
the way a fallen leaf dries.
Next the archipelago of scabs.
The clear plastic film of scar.
After a week, good as new.
Nine months ago, my father died.
Every day at least once but usually more
I think, *You are gone from this world*
where you lived all my life.
This unhealing—it seems a miracle.

Strays

I walk between downpours this overwet,
overwarm September, the swamp risen
into the farm road. Trees lean
as though they have spines that won't straighten.
Gnats by the hundreds drown on my skin,
stick there.

My father's latest stray, half-grown
half-Husky racing through puddles,
won't last long. They've taken stock—
the far buzzards circling.
They know the highway out front, its many scents,
its barreling log trucks and bored kids speeding.

Ahead not scat but a spill of grapes.
Limb overhanging, entwined—globe-heavy vine
(stray seed rooted, climbed)—purple muscadine.
I follow my footprints back, my cupped hands filled.
Smell them. My father hears with his eyes. *Eat.*
I mouth again: *eat.*

Wild juice baptizes our chins,
and we are born again.
My father's back straightens.
The highway refuses the stray.
Fingers grow sticky in bee-giddy arbors
of girlhood. Left with what's left, we spit out
sour pulp, bitter seed, crushed skin.

Phantom Limbs

The Hound

On display in the Acropolis Museum (Athens) is the damaged
sculpture of a guard dog to the Sanctuary of Artemis.

Among the ancients
long stripped of color
and emptied of scent,
throngs who do not threaten,
the marble hound crouches.
Ribs bare,
flank chiseled to bone,
he is kept hungry.
His nose—long, elegant, Egyptian—
knows our kind,
names each flushed pilgrim:
schoolboy, blond athlete,
plump woman of privilege.
Lost to the bite of time,
an ear, three legs.
Still, the muscles tense,
the single leonine paw
all but twitches.
Guard and hunter both,
he stays. That woman,
no athlete, much less immortal—
a thief of sites—sees
with the forbidden eye
of her camera past him
to the goddess, bow in hand,
washed beyond naked,
by centuries rendered invisible.
Centuries deep in his throat,
a growl gathers his phantom limbs,
arrows into a leap.

Yellow Dog

When they put her down,
I couldn't stand to watch.
My hand on the doorknob,
I turned.

Coughing rust,
she gathered what memory
lodged in her muscles, tensed
as though to follow.
Her amber eyes took in mine.

They gave her back to us
in a plastic bag, a black
trash bag in a cardboard box.

We drove her to a field,
a friend's camp; a foot down
hit red clay. It took till dark.
The bag was awkward—
seventy pounds, untensed.

Even now, years past rooms
unstartled by her barking,
past floors swept clean of her shedding,
I see her beneath latex hands
on that steel table

after the one night of her life
she refused to spend under our roof.
(We'd found her at dawn—
she couldn't stand—
in the backyard fort left to rot
by children who'd moved away.)

A lab coat's sheen,
the ceiling's fluorescent haze.
Only her eyes were in focus,
seeming to grasp in mine
her last command: Stay.
Compelled, for once, to obey.

Proof

The black dog settles his chin
on the edge of the bed,
works it onto my pillow.
He inches his nose-tip to mine
and breathes humid day
into my night-breath.
Canned sardines and damp Saltines.
Fumed out of dreaming,
I squint into his grave brown stare.
He needs to know that I will rise.
My hand finds his wide head,
a long soft ear. Satisfied,
he curls onto the floor,
begins at once to snore.

In this dim half-waking,
my spirit remembers fear
and cannot keep from returning
to the one child I was not unable
to bring into the world.
My face lowers, until—there—
her milkish breath, the rise and fall
of thin cotton, her rare small chest.
Holidays, she returns. As if a ghost,
I crack open her bedroom door.
Dark hair frames a woman's face,
but her mouth is her newborn mouth.
If she opens her eyes, she will laugh,
then she will leave.

Migrant Worker

Tolo, Greece

All day she emerges on the hour,
sweeps the flagstone patio
dividing hotel from beach—
Maria with the black plait
to her waist, face round and pretty and young.
Smiling into herself, she sweeps in time
to the small waves of the bay.
From on high, through balcony railings
painted blue to match the sea,
I pity her the Sisyphean task
and wonder at her smile,
until, looking out, I find
along the bar of the horizon
myself years ago, my daughter
beginning in my body.
Sand and pebbles return and return
on the unwashed feet of guests,
with wind or unexpected rain.
Nearby a pomegranate tree . . .
its flowers flaming, the fruit swelling.

Cyclades

At dusk, in mist, the islands fall apart
as dreams do at dawn, become ghosts that wander.
At dawn they find their bodies slowly,
as though hungover from too much young wine.
Slowly, they harden into shape like clay
in the kilns of artisans who paint designs,
wave-battered, wind-hammered rock—
the sky blue, the sea deeper blue,
the hills green and brown, the houses
of the people a glazed and blinding white.

Waterline

We sit on the porch at supper,
so homesick for the Atlantic,
we cast, catch, reel it west—
a thousand miles across 17, 95, and 20;
across the Pee Dee, Mississippi, and Red—

till sure enough, it smacks and thrashes
right over Shreveport, LA. Comes to rest
with the tide-swell of cicadas,
the hushbaby waves of wind
through heavy-leafed oaks
outside these old screens.

When they weep, the hawks turn into gulls.
Orange cannas break into flame—
tiki-torches from the 1960s, back
when our tans were deep, bodies lean,
feet sore from that trek on the shell-sharp waterline
from Huntington Beach to Litchfield
and, when the moon drank the tide down,
across to Pawleys Island. . . .

Sting of lemon on grilled trout,
crisp burnt skin. Just as we used to,
we cut the salt with gin.

Habitat

Who hasn't gotten drunk in a bar like this—
near a beach, maybe Florida, on spring break
or a business trip or post-divorce getaway?
Where the neon scrawl of Budweiser
or Coors Light, or the too-green shape of a palm tree
seeps through the dirty screen of cigarette smoke.

No long-expired license plates scale these walls,
no baseball caps on nails. Here,
strung-up fishing nets hold dried detritus—
seaweed, starfish, sand dollars. A mounted sailfish,
the five-foot shell of a loggerhead, a thing
like the blade of a chainsaw—you can't stop staring.

When the run-ragged bartender brings your fourth margarita,
you point: *What the hell?* She makes a gesture
that pretends to grow her nose.
And because the tequila has turned your brain
into an ecosystem swimming with trivia, you remember.
Sawfish: dinosaur. Around, you've read,
56 million years or more. "Critically endangered."

You know the type. A sun-blistered, soft-bellied jock
with a rod and reel and switchblade.
Nudged it one step closer toward "likely extinct."
In fact, there he sits, three stools over, downing shots.
Past time, you lift a fist-sized hunk of coral,
anchor your tip, veer toward the door.

Maybe it's the booze or maybe not. But you see clear
through the dingy air, the trophy-hung,
salt-damp walls—see the water rising, as though to take
all of it back—the Gulf set to a boil.

Ghost Net

Breeze-thrown seafoam,
breakers and swells . . .
The deep moans round
with many voices . . .
Stampedes of storms that fail
to rouse a soul, or so it seems,
to dead zones, red tides,
coral bleached to bone.
Whales—huge, confused—
heave ashore.

Beneath fever-laced blankets
of carbon, tributaries heavy
with fertilizer, pesticide,
industrial sludge—a riot of dreams.
Dynamite and cyanide,
longlines and trawling net,
gill, tangle, and drift net;
sweat-drenched dreams
of taking.

Leavings.
Mooring ropes, frayed, barnacled,
lash the oily shores of the Gulf.
Fishing lines knot
sea fans, sargassum, strap algae,
turtle grass—knot them
into bouquets, ceremonial decay.
Ghost nets,
forgotten by fishermen,

ride the waves, ripe
with rotting bycatch
and plastic—turtles, toothbrushes,
dolphins, flip-flops. Casting

and reeling its tides,
the sea aims
to hook open our eyes,
or so I might believe
if the living sea meant anything.

Earth Day

Post-Easter 2017

At the shoreline, soggy offal:
Life Savers, Skittles,
Jolly Ranchers, Dum Dums—
froot flavors and red dye #40
that sticks to cells till doomsday,
permanent as the plastic
ground in the gyres of the ocean,
or wound as filament in the bellies
of dead pelicans hard to spot
amid mounds of sargassum
here on the brown sand
of the Texas Gulf Coast
this April littered with pastel
halves of Dollar Store eggs,
their innards gobbled,
a sugar high for the sad-eyed Christ
who died so we don't have to,
who winged himself
unputrified the hell
away from here.

Goats on Sifnos

On the distant ridge—rocks. Until
at sunset they limp downhill as goats,
bawling, neck-bells clanking,
toward the dusty pen near the rental
where I nurse my empty stomach
with a bottle of dry Assyrtiko.
Injured, all? Hobbled, I see now they're closer,
right legs roped front to back. No danger
of running off, climbing too high,
or otherwise getting into trouble.
Later, in English, the taverna specialty:
Kid-in-a-Pot.

Fixing Junior

Easter at the Camp

We've pinned him down beside the barn
on a paint-scabbed bench.
In Michael's hand, a pocketknife.
No anesthesia. The screaming—
more child than goat.

Nancy grips his front legs,
Dave, the hind.
My hands press the ribs,
the kicking heart.
Marion holds his little horns.
Nick, who's ten, runs circles around us
and points: "Are they what hold the pee?"

Junior's eyes are filmy bulbs.
His shivery bleating rises. . . .
Once he goes quiet, limp as a rug,
we love him. "He's given up."
Marion shrugs. "He's ready to be eaten."
Michael's shirt is a red-brown Betadine Rorschach.
Junior's tongue is blue.
Mosquitoes, too early, shrill in our ears.
Mended with gauze and duct tape,
he blinks, wobbles to his feet,
climbs the hay bales straight up
to where they meet the roof.

They lie on a Bounty towel
on the bench, looking remarkably
like the eggs we hide—
first boiled, then dyed.

Performers

Walter B. Jacobs Memorial Nature Park

"They're more than birds," so says the ranger.
"This owl, this hawk.
These two, they are performers."

In their shared cage the barred owl,
feathery-fat, clacks its beak and fusses,
old-womanish, its talons sunk into something
small and furry and raw—mouse-ish—
pretending to forget to eat.
The red-tailed hawk, erect and still,
stares hard through smooth-sanded bars
as if caught by one thought:
This might be wood, but it isn't trees.

"They were hurt.
They can't survive out there."

Having gotten our fill of nature,
we forget them with the cranking
of our cars. Forget until the night when they,
whose memories are keen
and foreseeing, with beak and claw
whittle free and free-dive into our dreaming. Find
the bellies of our spaniels.
Hook out our eyes
and pluck from the roots for their nests
the hair of our sleeping children.

Bone Pit

That time, we pocketed arrowheads,
surprised a herd of deer, which raised white flags.
Your fingers traced a path through my sweat,
neck to shoulder, shoulder to wrist. We were twenty.

We're sixty. Our hands, though gloved, are ice.
Green lenses cover our eyes. We discuss ideas,
logos of the Stoics: the force of nature
that reconciles human and divine.

The road—unchanged. Hayfields to the west,
woods to the east. A hard wind shoves us down
into the swamp the hunters call Black Gum,
to the cross path marked by a disc harrow

whose nearly rusted-out seat holds two deer skulls.
Turn right, hit the bone pit, its stash of carcasses,
buzzards too busy to look up. We double back, shove
up into the wind. There, high-stepping

across the brown field close-mowed and baled—
buck, doe, fawn. In synchrony, they freeze, catch us
with their stare. Leap, freeze, leap,
straight through the hunters' camp and into the pines.

Our eyes water from such swift beauty.
From youth gone, yet not, even if at times
all we see are rusting harrows, buzzards, bones.
As though between us, deer invisibly rustle.

Notes and Dedications

"*Homo naledi*." The fossils of *Homo naledi* (Star Man) were eventually dated to a relatively recent 236,000 to 335,000 years ago. *H. naledi*, apparently existing alongside larger-brained hominins, is not thought to be a direct ancestor of modern humans, although it is probably an offshoot within the genus *Homo* (BBC, May 9, 2017).

"Tour of Grief." From July 24 to August 9, 2018, scientists observed Tahlequah (J35), a southern resident killer whale in the Pacific Northwest, carrying the carcass of her newborn calf—a record-breaking "tour of grief." For the previous three years, no calf had survived among these orcas—all of whom suffer from malnutrition, thanks to pollution and the demise of Chinook salmon, their main food source. . . . During the spring of 2018, the U.S. government began forcibly separating families seeking asylum at the southern border.

"Babyland." Many cemeteries have an area reserved for stillbirths, infants, and small children, commonly known as Babyland.

"Hand-Knit." This poem borrows from the title of a short story by Amy Hempel: "Beg, Sl Tog, Inc, Cont, Rep."

"Ghost Net." This poem was written in response to *Global Contamination: A Gulf Project,* a mixed-media installation by Joan Hall. The two italicized lines are from Tennyson's "Ulysses."

"Perseids," for Dorie LaRue.

"Diving before Dawn," for Cayman Brac Shore Divers.

"Grandmother Faceless," for Marguerite Hall Mace.

"Beach Music," for Eunice Fearrington Prescott.

"Prayer Flags," for Karen Swenson.

"Bone Pit," for David Havird.

CPSIA information can be obtained
at www.ICGtesting.com
Printed in the USA
LVHW091309180321
681854LV00005B/133